清 东 陵

The Eastern Qing Tombs

中国世界语出版社出版 北京

PUBLISHED BY CHINA ESPERANTO PRESS, BEIJING

First edition 1997

ISBN 7-5052-0304-5

Published by China Esperanto Press, Beijing
24 Baiwanzhuang Road, Beijings 100037, China
Distributed by China International Book Trading Corporation
35 Chegongzhuang Xilu, Beijing 100044, China
P.O. Box 399, Beijing, China

Printed in the People's Republic of China

清东陵是清王朝(公元 1644－1911 年)入关后开辟的第一座皇帝、皇后陵区。它位于北京迤东 125 公里的河北省遵化市马兰峪境内，是中国现存规模最大、体系最完整的古代帝王后妃陵墓群，全国重点文物保护单位和著名的风景名胜旅游区。

清东陵始建于顺治十八年(1661 年)，共有帝、后、妃和公主陵寝 15 座。其中有清朝入关第一帝顺治的孝陵，第二帝康熙的景陵，第四帝乾隆的裕陵，第七帝咸丰的定陵，第八帝同治的惠陵；还有孝庄、孝惠、孝贞(慈安)、孝钦(慈禧)4 座皇后陵；景妃、景双妃、裕妃、定妃、惠妃等 5 座妃园寝。从时间和人数上看，从 1663 年葬入顺治皇帝起，至 1935 年葬入同治皇帝的最后一位皇贵妃止，历时 272 年，共葬 161 人。

整个清东陵陵区，占地 2500 平方公里，分后龙和前圈两个部分。

陵寝后龙，是风水来龙之地，它从陵后长城开始，向北经过清东陵的少祖山雾灵山，蜿蜒起伏，延伸到承德附近，西端与密云县接壤，东面则直达遵化州城。整个后龙地带山峦起伏，群峰叠翠，奇峰秀岭，纵横交结，风景异常秀丽。

前圈部分是陵寝所在地，占地 48 平方公里，南面以大红门为起点，东西分别建有风水墙，总长达四十余华里。风水墙随山就势，东侧经马兰峪向北，直达马兰关，与长城相接；西侧横跨西大河，越过高低错落的丘陵，径抵黄花山南麓，围护着陵区的安全。

中国历代帝王陵寝，均强调"风水"，用现代的意思说，即自然环境。中国风水术源远流长，历代风水学家概括出一个"风水宝地"的环境模式：其北有连绵高山为屏障，南有远山近丘遥相呼应，左右两侧有低岭环护，内有广阔平原，河流穿坼蜿蜒流去。这个模式被称为"四神地"或"四灵地"，是阳宅、阴宅皆追求的理想境界。

清东陵陵址的选择，强调"总以地臻全美为重"，力求符合中国传统"风水"模式。整个清东陵北靠层峦叠翠的昌瑞山，东依马兰峪蜿蜒起伏的鹰飞倒仰山，西傍蓟县高耸入云的黄花山，南抵天然翠屏、宛若倒扣金钟的金星山。更南为象山、烟墩两山对峙，形成一个险峻的陵口，名叫兴隆口，整个陵区之水汇集于此，直泻淋河。是典型的"四神地"。

万年吉地选中以后，须按规制营建一系列建筑，其总体布局与皇宫无异，大体为"前朝后寝"。加上前边长长的神道，形成庞大而森严的建筑群体。

所谓神道，系指通向祭殿和坟前的导引大道，以壮观瞻。帝陵前均有神道，但每一陵区内仅有一条主神道，即首帝陵前的神道。清东陵的主神道是孝陵神道。其余为次神道，规模较小，接在主神道上，称作"以次接主"。整个陵区由神道连接成一个整体。明清时期的神道可谓发展到了顶点，清东陵仅孝陵神道就长达5公里。

在神道上，要依次排列一些礼仪性建筑。清东陵神道建筑和石刻依次为：石牌坊、大红门、具服殿、神功圣德碑亭、影壁山、石望柱、石像生、龙凤门、七孔桥，等等。

其次为祭祀建筑区，这是陵园地面建筑的主体部分，供祭祀之用。清东陵的祭祀建筑大致为：神道碑亭、神厨库、朝房（祭祀时烧制奶茶、制做面食的地方）、值房（守陵人住宿之处）、隆恩门、焚帛炉、东西配殿、隆恩殿、三孔桥、陵寝门、二柱门、石五供等。

再就是封土，即坟上的土堆。其建筑方法是在地宫上砌筑高大的砖城，城内填土，使之高出城墙形成一圆顶。城墙上设垛口和女墙，宛如一座小城。这城墙称为"宝城"，高出的圆顶叫"宝顶"。宝城前尚有一突出的方形城台，上建明楼，称为"方城明楼"，楼内竖立墓主的陵号碑，作为某陵寝的标志。方城明楼与宝城宝顶是结合为一体的建筑，从方城正中开券洞，进洞后有一哑巴院，又名月牙城，然后从此城两侧上下。

宝城宝顶和方城明楼构成的坟头，突出地显示了陵寝的庄严气氛，也增强了建筑的艺术效果。

最后是地下宫殿。地宫是帝后陵寝的重要部分，又叫"玄宫"、"幽宫"等，因其结构豪华富丽，堪与帝王的人间宫殿媲美，俗称地下宫殿。由于地宫是埋葬帝后身骨和殉葬大量珍宝之处，过去不为世人所知，所以一直是个谜。现在有明定陵、清东陵裕陵、慈禧陵地宫作参照，才解开了这个千古之谜。

清东陵裕陵地宫是无梁无柱的拱券式结构，由墓道券、闪当券、罩门券、明堂券、穿堂券、金券及三个门洞券等九券和四道石门组成，进深 54 米，总面积达 372 平方米，所有券顶和四周石壁，满布佛教题材的雕刻。它不仅是一座不可多得的石雕艺术宝库，又是一座庄严肃穆的地下佛堂。

地宫石门上的门楼，是用整块青白石雕琢的，出檐瓦垄、兽吻横梁，都刻得十分精致。门楼上方的月光石半圆形内，雕有佛像、执壶、孔雀翎、海螺等吉祥器物。在地宫的四道石门上，按照皇陵地宫石作的规制，浮雕着八尊菩萨的立像。他们身高约 1.5 米，都妆扮得异常优美。在券壁、券顶上，还雕刻着四大天王、五方佛、五欲供、八宝等图案，他们护佑着地宫，使亡灵安然自得地进入极乐世界。

金券是地宫最后的堂券，为主要墓室，在宽 12 米的艾叶青石宝床正中，停放着乾隆皇帝的棺椁。两侧为两位随葬皇后和三位皇贵妃的灵柩。乾隆帝棺下有一口"金眼吉井"，相传这口井是不竭不溢的。实际上井口直径只有十多厘米，仅是一个"穴位"，井中无水，其中曾随葬了乾隆皇帝生前喜爱的珍宝。金券顶部刻有三大朵佛花，外层为二十四个花瓣，花心由梵文和佛像组成。佛周围簇拥着珊瑚、火珠等吉祥器物。金券东西壁平水墙上，半圆的月光石里，刻着佛像和八宝图案。平水墙下，所有围墙上都刻满了梵、藏两种文字的阴刻经咒。它们编排严密，端庄整齐，刀法遒劲有力。

特别值得一提的是帝后陵的殉葬。殉葬的本意大约有两点：一是作为纪念性，表达生者感情上对死者的怀念；二是灵魂观念所引起的，认为人死后到另一个世界去，仍过着同人世间一样的生活，也需要生产工具、日用品和爱好的玩物。为了使死者在"阴间"过得如同"阳间"一样美好，使用殉葬的方式把这些东西送给他们。由于中国数千年来奉行厚葬，历代统治阶级均把大量财富埋进坟墓。除金银财宝外，还有数量可观的日用器物、工艺美术品等，称得上是一座座地下宝库。

裕陵地宫仅乾隆帝装殓的随葬品就有佛字台正珠珠顶冠、绣黄宁绸锦金龙袍、珊瑚嘛呢字朝珠、绣黄缎三等正珠豆子荷包等若干文物，如果加上梓宫中随葬的东西，其奢华靡费令人咋舌。

清东陵优美的环境，精美的建筑，珍贵的文物，完备的体制，无一不为我们认识清朝的历史提供了宝贵的实物佐证。

The Eastern Qing Tombs, the first imperial cemetery the Qing Dynasty built after the Manchus crossed the Great Wall and entered Beijing, are located at Malanyu in Zunhua City in Hebei Province, 125 kilometres east of Beijing. They are one of the best preserved burial grounds in China, an important state-protected cultural site, and a well-known scenic attraction for tourists.

The construction of the Eastern Qing Tombs began in the eighteenth year of the Shun Zhi Reign (1661). All together 15 imperial tombs were built here including five for emperors: Xiaoling for Emperor Shun Zhi, the first emperor of the Qing Dynasty after the regime was established in Beijing; Jingling for Emperor Kang Xi, the second emperor; Yuling for Emperor Qian Long, the fourth emperor; Dingling for Emperor Xian Feng, the seventh emperor; and Huiling for Emperor Tong Zhi, the eighth emperor. There are four for the empresses Xiao Zhuang, Xiao Hui, Xiao Zhen (Ci An) and Xiao Xin (Ci Xi), five for imperial concubines Jingfei, Jingshuangfei, Yufei, Dingfei and Huifei, and one for princess. It took 272 years from 1663 when Emperor Shun Zhi was buried to 1935 when the last imperial concubine was interred to complete, and all together 161 people were buried in this large cemetery.

The Eastern Qing Tombs cover a total area of 2,500 square kilometres and consist of two parts: the Rear Dragon and the Front Site.

The Rear Dragon starts from the Great Wall behind the tombs and runs through the Shaozu and Wuling mountains to Chengde in the north, borders Miyun County to the west and extends to the city of Zunhua on the east side. With undulating high mountain peaks rising one after another, and grotesque rocks standing here and there, the area is of great beauty.

The Front Site, where the cemetery lies, covers an area of 48 square kilometres. It starts from the Grand Palace Gate in the south, with a surrounding wall on the eastern and western sides totalling 20 kilometres. The surrounding wall runs northward along the ranging mountain slopes through Malanyu to Malanguan to connect with the Great Wall on the east and across the Xida River to pass through the hills to the southern side of the Huanghua Mountain on the west, providing a protective wall for the entire cemetery.

The imperial burial grounds are closely related to the "Feng-shui", or the natural topographical features of the area. The practice of Fengshui appeared very early in China. Geomancers of the past dynasties developed a concept for an ideal residence for both the living and the dead: mountains to the near north serve as shelter, mountains to the far south as a response to the mountains in the north, low hills on the right and left sides as guards, broad flat land on the site, and rivers flowing nearby. Such a place was called "land of four divinities" or "land of four spirits".

To tally with this traditional Chinese theory of Fengshui, geomancers bore in mind the instruction that "the best location must be chosen" when they went to conduct surveys of the site. The Eastern Qing Tombs have the Changrui Mountain Peaks rising one higher than another on the north, the undulating Yingfeidaoyang Mountains in the east, the high Huanghua Mountains to the west and the natural screen-like Jinxing Mountains to the south. Further south Xiangshan and Yandun form an entrance to the cemetery which is called Xinlingkou and to which all the water in the vicinity flows to form the Xida River. It is a typical "land of four divinities".

Once the site was decided upon, a series of structures would be erected. They would be arranged as those in the imperial palace: with an outer court for the emperor to handle state affairs and an inner court as living quarters. A long path called "Sacred Way" led to the entrance of the tomb.

A main Sacred Way to the head tomb (the oldest) and subsidiary Sacred Ways to lesser tombs are always found in an imperial cemetery. The main Sacred Way of the Eastern Qing Tombs is the one to Xiaoling. The subsidiary Sacred Ways are connected to the main one, and they form an integral whole in the cemetery. The Sacred Ways reached a height of development in the Ming and Qing dynasties, and the Sacred Way of Xiaoling is five kilometres long. Along the Sacred Ways are a stone archway, Grand Palace Gate, the Hall for Changing Clothes, Divine Merits Stele Tower, Screen Hill (an earth mound to block direct view to the tomb), stone columns, stone sculptures, the Dragon-Phoenix Gate and Seven-arch Bridge.

The buildings at the end of a Sacred Way are for sacrificial ceremonies. The ceremonial structures in the Eastern Qing Tombs are arranged in this order: Stele Tower on the Sacred Way, Kitchen Storehouse, Pastry Room, Guardhouse, Long'en Gate, Sacrificial Paper Burner, Wing Halls on the east and west, Long'en Hall, Three-Arch Bridge, Gate to the Burial Mound, Double-Pillar Gate and the Five Stone Altar Pieces.

Usually an imperial tomb is constructed in the following way: after the burial chamber is completed, a high and thick wall is built to go around the chamber that rises higher than the ground level, the earth is piled inside the wall to form a mound with its top higher than the wall. The wall-enclosed area is called the "Precious Citadel" and the mound is called the "Precious Top". The high wall is complete with battlements and crenels. There is a square walled area in front of each tomb called "Square City". A tower on top of it houses a stone tablet inscribed with the deceased emperor's posthumous title. The tower, integrated with the "Precious Top" in structure, can be reached by two ramps either inside or outside the wall.

The high earth mound and the tower on top of the Square City greatly enhance the solemnity and grandeur of the imperial burial ground.

The mammoth burial chamber, known as the "Underground Palace", is comparable to the palaces for the emperors in its extravagant design and decoration. Many objects were buried along with the dead emperor. These "Underground Palaces" were mysterious to the common people in the past, but after Dingling of the Ming Tombs, and Yuling and Empress Ci Xi's tomb of the Eastern Qing Tombs were opened up, they are not so mysterious today.

The Underground Palace of Yuling of the Eastern Qing Tombs is an arched structure without pillars or beams. Fifty-four metres below the surface, the 372-square-metre ground is composed of nine vaults and four stone gates, with Buddhist engravings on all ceilings and walls. It is not only a great artistic treasure-house but also an underground Buddhist hall.

The front gatetower is carved out of a whole piece of white marble. The eaves gutters and animal beams are exquisitely carved. The semicircle Moonbeam Stone on top of the gatetower is carved with auspicious objects such as Buddhist images, pots, peacock feather and conches. Carved on the fourth stone gate are eight relief images of Bodhisattva. About 1.5 metres high, they are beautifully clad. On the vault's walls and ceiling are the images of Four Deva-Kings and other Buddhist figures.

The Burial Chamber is the last vault and main part of the Underground Palace. In it the coffin of Emperor Qian Long is placed in the middle of the 12-metre-wide marble bed. On either side of the emperor's coffin are the coffins of two empresses and three imperial concubines. Beneath the coffin of Emperor Qian Long is an auspicious well. It was said that the well never went dry or flooded. In fact the well with a diameter of only ten centimetres in the mouth serves as "an auspicious point" for the tomb and has no water in it. Buried in it were treasures belonging to the emperor when he was alive. On the ceiling of the vault are engraved three large Buddhist flowers with 24 petals. In the centre of the flowers are Sanskrit and Buddhist images surrounded by corals and pearls. Engraved on the semicircle Moonbeam Stones on the eastern and western walls are also Buddhist images and Eight-Treasure patterns. At the foot of walls are Buddhist scriptures engraved in intaglio in Sanskrit and the Tibetan language. The engravings are neat and very powerful.

Of particular interest are the sacrificial objects in the imperial tombs. People in ancient times believed that the dead would lead a life much similar to that of the living. They would need production implements, articles for daily use and things for entertainment, so these things were buried along with the dead. Emperors, royal family members, the rich and high-ranking officials in the several thousand years of feudal society took numerous articles of daily use, arts and crafts, jewellery, and other things with them to their burial grounds. Every large tomb is an underground treaures-house.

Objécts buried with Emperor Qian Long in the underground palace are numerous. They include a gold crown with pearls, a robe embroidered with dragons in gold, pearls, silk purses, etc.

In a word, the Eastern Qing Tombs have beautiful surroundings, exquisite buildings and numerous cultural relics. The place is not only a scenic attraction for tourists but provides valuable materials for the study of Qing history.

蓬莱仙境 清东陵风光旖旎，景色秀丽。晴日的清晨，云雾缭绕，碧水白桥，黄瓦红墙与苍松翠柏交相辉映，疑入蓬莱仙境。这里是人文美与自然美有机结合的风景胜地。

A Fairyland   The cemetery of the Eastern Qing Tombs is a scenic place. After morning clouds and mists have scattered, blue rivers, white bridges, golden roofs, red walls and green pine and cypress trees appear to form a beautiful picture. People took this place for a fairyland.

15

顺治皇帝画像 顺治皇帝(1644—1661年在位),名爱新觉罗.福临,年号顺治,庙号世祖,是清朝入关后第一位皇帝。他执政期间,努力发展生产,促进满汉各民族的融合,对于清初社会稳定和进步起到了积极的作用。

Portrait of Emperor Shun Zhi Emperor Shun Zhi (reigned 1644-61), named Fu Lin, was the first Qing emperor after the Manchus took Beijing. During his reign, he promoted production and the unity of various nationalities, playing an active role in stabilizing the society in the early period of the Qing Dynasty.

孝陵全景 为清东陵首陵,居陵区中轴线,是清顺治皇帝、孝康章皇后和孝献皇后的陵寝。它从石牌坊开始,全长5600米,由大小28组建筑物组成,是陵区规模最大、体系最完整的陵寝,成为清朝入关后各帝陵的蓝本。

A Panoramic View of Xiaoling The oldest of the Eastern Qing Tombs on the central axis is for Emperor Shun Zhi and his empresses Xiaokang Zhang and Xiao Xian. Starting from the Stone Archway, it is 5,600 metres long and consists of 28 groups of buildings. The largest of Eastern Qing Tombs, the tomb served as an example for all consequent imperial tombs after the Manchus took Beijing.

石牌坊　孝陵第一座建筑,它标志着陵区的开始。牌坊通体由汉白玉石料雕刻而成,宽 31.35 米,高 12.48 米,五门六柱十一楼,是中国现存石牌坊中最宽的一座。

Stone Archway　The first structure on the approach to Xiaoling, the archway of white marble is 31.35 metres wide and 12.48 metres high. Six pillars divide the gate into five openings. It is the widest stone archway extant in China.

石牌坊斗栱 斗栱，是中国木结构建筑中的支承构件，可使屋檐较大程度外伸，是中国传统建筑造型的一个重要特征。石牌坊上斗栱采用木结构手法，用石料雕刻而成，玲珑剔透，富有美感。

Dougong on the Stone Archway *Dougong*, a system of brackets inserted between the top of a column and a crossbeam in wood structures, protracts the eaves. It is an important feature of traditional Chinese architecture. The *dougong* on this Stone Archway is carved out of stone and is very exquisite.

夹柱石浮雕 石牌坊每根石柱下部设夹柱石两块，均装饰着浮雕图案，中间两块夹柱石雕刻着云龙戏珠图案。祥云中玉龙升腾，身体曲张有致，一颗火珠，呼呼生风。整幅雕刻充满生气和活力。

Stone Relief Carvings Each of the pillars of the Stone Archway has two pieces of stones at its base carved in relief with the motif of the dragons playing with pearls among drifting clouds. The motifs are very beautiful.

大红门 位于石牌坊北,是孝陵门户,也是清东陵的总门户。门分三洞,为东陵现存建筑中唯一的一座庑殿顶建筑。两侧连接着环绕整个陵区的风水围墙。

Grand Palace Gate It is the front gate to Xiaoling and the main entrances to the whole ground of Eastern Qing Tombs. It is the only gate in this imperial cemetery without a gate tower. A high wall stretches from the gate to enclose the whole area.

具服殿 位于大红门内东侧,是皇帝谒陵时更衣之所。院内建单檐歇山式殿宇三间,皇帝在这里更换素衣后,才能进入陵区祭祀。

Hall for Changing Clothes Located on the eastern side of the Grand Palace Gate, this hall was the place where emperors changed clothes when they came to offer sacrifices to their ancestors. Only after they changed to plain clothes could they enter the cemetery. With single eaves and a gabled roof, the hall has three bays.

神功圣德碑亭 俗称大碑楼,是一座纪念性建
筑物。碑亭四隅各竖汉白玉石华表一座,如辰
星拱卫,庄重肃穆。楼内正中由神兽赑屃托起
石碑一统,其上用满汉两种文字记载着顺治帝
的文治武功。

Divine Merit Stele Tower   A commemorative building, the Stele Tower has marble stone columns on
its four corners. Inside it is a stone stele on an animal with an inscription written in Manchu and Chinese languages recording the achievements made by
Emperor Shun Zhi during his lifetime.

望柱 在陵寝前建望柱作为神道入口标志,始于南朝时期(公元 420 – 589 年)。宋代(公元 960 – 1279 年)以后退居到次要位置,仅作为石像生的起始标志。图中孝陵望柱满刻云纹,纹饰端庄,刀法隽秀,为石雕艺术的上乘之作。

Wangzhu The stone column was a mark of entrance to a burial ground. It originated from the Southern Dynasty (420-589 AD). Before the end of the Song Dynasty (960-1279) it was placed at the beginning of a Sacred Way. During the Ming and Qing dynasties a stone archway replaced its original function, and *wangzhu* became a purely ornamental object lying before stone sculptures. This *wangzhu* from Xiaoling carved with cloud designs in relief is a masterpiece of stone sculpture for its delicate workmanship.

石像生 为一组石人石兽雕刻。帝陵前设石像生，始于秦汉(公元前221－公元220年)，用以表饰坟垅，象征死者生前仪卫。孝陵石像生共十八对，由南向北井然有序地排列着狮子、狻猊、骆驼、大象、麒麟、马，卧立各一对；武将、文臣各三对。其雕刻技法古朴粗犷，表现出清初艺术的写意风格。

Stone Sculptures The custom to place stone sculptures in imperial cemeteries began in the Qin Dynasty (221-206 BC) and the Han Dynasty (206 BC-AD 220) to serve as ceremonial guards. Stone sculptures in front of Xiaoling are 18 pairs arranged in a row from south to north: lions, *suani*, camels, elephants, unicorns, horses, and army generals and civil officials. The animals either stand or crouch. Six pairs are of human figures. They represent the best sculptural achievements of the early Qing Dynasty.

武将 整体造型古朴敦厚,面部表情似笑非笑,于和蔼中隐含刚猛之气,显示出清初八旗大将的凛凛雄风。

Army Generals The military officers have an expression with a subdued smile, hiding their fierceness in mildness. The sculptures describe army generals of the Manchu in the early days, who had preserved many of their original nomadic characteristics.

大象 它温顺,又是力量的象征,置于神道,寓意皇帝广有顺民。孝陵大象,体形刚健,形象逼真,雕刻风格豪放,无造作之感。

Elephants The docile animal is a symbol of strength in China. It is placed on the Sacred Way to imply that the emperor abode by the wishes of the common people. The elephants at Xiaoling are powerful and lifelike.

龙凤门 明陵称"棂星门"。棂星即天田星,故棂星门即天之门,进入此门即寓意进入天国。此门横亘石像生北端,亦有收束视线,避免目光所及空旷无际的作用。

Dragon-Phoenix Gate It was called Lingxing Gate in the Ming Dynasty, a gate leading to Heaven. It stands at the northern end of the Stone Sculptures to block the direct view.

神道碑亭 为重檐歇山式建筑。内有石碑一统，其上用满、蒙、汉三种文字刻着顺治皇帝的庙号和谥号全称。孝陵陵院建筑自此开始。

Stele Pavilion of Xiaoling
The pavilion on the Sacred Way of Xiaoling has a gabled roof. A stone tablet in it bears the posthumous title of Emperor Shun Zhi. The pavilion stands at the beginning of the Xiaoling compound.

隆恩门　是陵院正门,面阔五间,进深二间,单
檐歇山式建筑。前开三洞大门,中门稍宽,叫神
门,供帝后梓宫通行;左为君门,供皇帝祭奠时
出入;右为臣门,王公大臣由此通行。隆恩门两
侧连接着环绕整座陵院的红墙。

Long'en Gate This gate in the middle of the Sacred
Way has a gabled roof and three openings. The
central opening is wider, through which the coffin
of the deceased emperor was carried to the burial
chamber. The opening on the left was used by the
living emperor and the opening on the right was
used by court officials. The wall to enclose the
compound begins on either side of the gate.

西配殿壁画 西配殿位于隆恩门北、隆恩殿前西侧,是帝后忌辰喇嘛念经的地方。孝陵西配殿内壁画,再现了顺治时期的政治、军事、宫廷生活等社会风云。图为局部,表现的是顺治九年(1652 年)世祖在西苑隆重接见达赖五世(1617－1682 年)的情景。这次接见,密切了清王朝与蒙、藏等少数民族间的关系。

Wall Painting in the Western Wing Hall The Western Wing Hall to the north of Long'en Gate and to the west of Long'en Hall was where Buddhist monks held services for the deceased emperor and empresses. A painting on the wall inside it depicts the scene when Emperor Shun Zhi received the fifth Dalai Lama in 1652 in Beijing. This meeting strengthened relations between the central government and the Mongolian and Tibetan people.

从明楼俯瞰隆恩殿　隆恩殿亦称享殿,为重檐
歇山式建筑,是放置帝后牌位和举行祭祀仪式
的主要地方。

Long'en Hall Viewed from the Memorial Tower　Also
called the Offerings Hall, this hall has double eaves
and a gabled roof. It was used to keep memorial
tablets with deceased emperor's name on them and
hold sacrificial ceremonies.

鼎式炉 陈设于隆恩殿前月台上,炉有双耳,三足为狻猊头;炉盖重檐,圆形攒尖,顶置宝珠。每遇祭奠,炉内燃香,烟雾缥缈。

***Ding*-Style Incense Burner** The bronze burner on the marble terrace of Long'en Hall has two handles and three legs decorated with the head of *suanni*. The lid tapers upward in several tiers with a ball on top. At sacrificial ceremonies incense was burned in it.

孝东陵　位于孝陵东 0.5 公里处,是清朝第一座皇后陵,内葬孝惠章皇后及顺治帝的 28 名妃嫔。此陵开创了清朝皇后单独建陵之制,形成了清代皇后陵的基本格局。但体制不完善,将妃嫔也葬入陵内,构成皇后陵兼妃园寝的形式。陵园内孝惠章皇后宝顶前建方城明楼,明楼东西两侧纵向各排两行妃嫔宝顶,形成以皇后宝顶为中心,群星拱卫,唯我独尊的格局。

Eastern Xiaoling　Located 0.5 kilometre from Xiaoling, this was the first tomb built for empresses in the Qing Dynasty. It houses the remains of Empress Xiaohui Zhang and 28 concubines of Emperor Shun Zhi. It set a precedent for building tombs exclusively for the emperor's wives. A tower stands on the Square City in front of the highest earth mound, under which the two empresses are buried. Imperial concubines are buried under the earth mounds on either side of the large mound.

康熙皇帝画像 康熙皇帝（1662－1722年在位），名爱新觉罗.玄烨，年号康熙，庙号圣祖，清入关后第二位皇帝，是中国在位时间最长的封建帝王。他在位期间，平三藩、三次亲征蒙古准噶尔部噶尔丹叛乱、统一台湾、安定西藏、六下江南，文治武功均达到了很高成就，开创了中国历史上著名的"康乾盛世"。

Portrait of Emperor Kang Xi' Emperor Kang Xi (reigned 1662-1722) was the second emperor after the Manchus established their regime in Beijing. His was the longest reign in China. During his reign he put down rebellions, went on expeditions, unified Taiwan, pacified Tibet and toured southern China six times. He made great achievements in all fields and thus began the famous "Kang-Qian Prosperous Period" in Chinese history.

景陵 为清康熙皇帝陵寝，祔葬孝诚仁皇后等四后一皇贵妃。景陵规模宏大，布局集中，建筑工艺精美，并首创双碑、牌楼门等形式。它在丧制上也有所改革，皇后先入地宫以待皇帝和帝陵中安葬皇贵妃，均由景陵首创。

Jingling This is the tomb of Emperor Kang Xi and four empresses and one imperial concubine. The tomb was the first to have two stone memorial tablets and a front gate like a palace hall. The complex is large in scale and beautifully designed

华表 矗立于大碑亭四隅,用汉白玉石雕成,高达十余米,柱身雕刻一条腾云驾雾的蛟龙,龙体屈曲盘旋,奋力争腾,寓动于静,栩栩如生。

Stone Column On each of the four corners of the Grand Stele Tower stands a ten-metre high stone column carved out of white marble. The stone column is engraved with a dragon coiling up through clouds. The engraved dragon and clouds are very lifelike.

五孔桥 雄跨于大碑楼北,桥长 107 米,宽十余米,如长虹卧波,气势雄伟。景陵五孔桥在东陵各桥中最为壮观,其石质之精良,石料之宽阔,实属罕见。

Five-Arch Bridge Located on the northern side of the Grand Stele Tower, the stone bridge is 107 metres long and more than ten metres wide, and looks like a rainbow over billowing waters. The five-arch bridge of Jingling is the most magnificent among the bridges in the Eastern Qing Tombs.

神道 即墓道。由于受河流的影响，景陵神道修成弯曲的，五对石像生也随着神道的曲折布置在神路两侧。在弯曲的神路上布置石像生，在清代陵寝中仅此一例。

Sacred Way The Sacred Way of Jingling curves in line with the river. Five pairs of stone sculptures are arranged along this winding way. Among the Qing tombs, this is the only Sacred Way with stone sculptures at its bends.

石象 是清帝陵前不可少的一种石像生。景陵石象，与清初自然古朴的雕刻风格不同，显得奢华和造作。它饰有鞍鞯，驮起宝瓶，称为"太平有象"，寓意国泰民安。

Stone Elephants Stone elephants were indispensable for the stone sculptures in front of the Qing tombs. The stone elephants in front of Jingling differ from the natural and primitive style of engraving in the early Qing. They are decorated with saddles and treasure bottles on their back representing peace in the country.

33

隆恩门 景陵两侧山峰苍翠欲滴,周围河流水源丰富。红墙黄瓦、彩画鲜艳的隆恩门,在阳光照耀下,泛起万点金辉,倒映在波纹激滟的马槽沟中,既增加了景观深度,又与湖光山色融为一体,使人流连忘返。

Long'en Gate The emerald mountains lie on either side of Jingling, and a river runs around it. The Long'en Gate, with its yellow tile roof and red walls, looks magnificent under the sunshine.

明楼 为陵寝标志,建在宝城正前方,座落于方城之上,是整个陵寝的制高点。楼为重檐歇山式,上有匾额,额曰"景陵"。内有陵号碑,上刻"圣祖仁皇帝之陵"七个径尺大字。

Memorial Tower The tower on top of the "Square City" in front of the earth mound is the mark of an imperial burial place. It has double eaves and a gabled roof. Above the gate of the tower is a plaque inscribed with the tomb's name: "Jingling", and inside the tower is a stone tablet inscribed with "Tomb of Benevolent Emperor Sheng Zu". Each character is about 33 centimetres square.

龙椅 摆放在皇帝陵隆恩殿内,供安设神牌之用。每逢大祭,龙椅置于供案前正中,其上安设皇帝神牌,皇后神牌则安放在分列两侧的凤椅上,皇贵妃凤椅另在旁位。

Dragon Chair The chair is placed inside the Long'en Hall with the emperor's tablet on it. At memorial ceremony the chair was put in the centre of the hall behind the sacrificial table, and tablets of the empresses and imperial concubines were put on the Phoenix Chairs on either side of it.

景陵皇贵妃园寝 俗称双妃园寝，位于景陵东南1公里处，内葬康熙皇帝的两个妃子。这两位妃子曾抚育过幼年的乾隆皇帝弘历，所以弘历即位后于乾隆四年(1739年)为二妃单独建立了园寝。图为园寝宫门外的单孔拱桥。

Tombs of Imperial Concubines Located one kilometre to the southeast of Jingling, the tombs hold the remains of Emperor Kang Xi's two concubines who had brought the young emperor up. After Emperor Qian Long was enthroned, he had the special tomb built for them. The picture shows the single-arch bridge in front of the tomb's palace gate.

配殿 双妃园寝等级较高，较一般妃园寝增建了东西配殿、方城明楼。图为西配殿，上覆绿色琉璃瓦，说明它的等级低于帝后陵。

Wing Hall The two imperial concubines' tomb has two wing halls and a front tower, an addition to the tomb exceeding the status of imperial concubines. But the halls have roofs made of glazed tiles in green colour, which shows that the tomb is inferior to that of the empresses.

丹陛石 设于陵寝隆恩殿前，是等级的象征，示尊严之意。双妃园寝丹陛石上刻"丹凤朝阳"图案，丹凤独立山石，口衔灵芝，仰望旭日；漫天祥云缭绕，海水抃崖，气势宏伟。在妃园寝设丹陛石，清陵仅此一处。

Stone Stairs The stone stairs in front of the Long'en Hall are a symbol of status and dignity. The stone stairs before the tomb of the two imperial concubines are called "A Phoenix Faces the Sun". It describes a phoenix standing on a rock and holding glossy ganderma in its beak, looking toward the red sun rising through auspicious clouds from the billowing sea. Only this tomb has such stone stairs in the Qing tombs.

裕陵　清朝入关后第四代皇帝乾隆的陵
寝。乾隆年间国库充盈,兴建裕陵历时
五十余年,其规模、质量在清帝陵中均属
上乘。

Yuling It is the tomb of Qian Long, the
fourth emperor of the Qing Dynasty after
the Manchus set up their regime in Beijing.
The construction of this tomb continued for
over 50 years. It is one of the best and the
largest of Qing tombs.

双妃园寝明楼　园寝内两座绿色琉璃瓦盖顶的明楼东西并列，在晚霞映衬下尤显俊俏。

Memorial Towers　The two memorial towers of the two imperial concubines' tomb have roofs with green glazed tiles. They stand facing each other in the setting sun.

乾隆皇帝戎装像 乾隆皇帝(1736－1795年在位)，名爱新觉罗.
弘历，年号乾隆，庙号高宗。他25岁登基，在位60年，又当了3年
太上皇，89岁去世，是中国封建社会实际执政时间最长、享寿最高
的皇帝。乾隆年间，清朝的政治、军事、文化都得到了空前的发展，
封建经济达到了鼎盛时期。

Portrait of Emperor Qian Long   Emperor Qian Long (reigned 1736-95)
ascended to the throne at 25, where he remained for the next 60 years.
He retired to become the Super-Sovereign for three years before he died
at the age of 89. He ruled and lived the longest among the Chinese emperors. During his reign unprecedented development took place in the
politics, the military and culture, and feudal economy enjoyed the period of greatest prosperity in China.

裕陵双碑 圣德神功碑建双碑始于康熙景陵。乾隆皇帝在位年久,文治武功,显赫一时,号称"十全老人"。为彰其德,亦立双碑,左满文,右汉文。碑文由嘉庆帝御撰,字体由乾隆第十一子、清代著名书法家成亲王永瑆书写,洋洋洒洒,二千余字,极尽歌功颂德之能事。

Twin Steles of Yuling China was in peace and prosperity in the reign of Emperor Qian Long. To sing praises for him, Emperor Jia Qing wrote a eulogy, and Prince Yong Xing, a famous calligrapher and the eleventh son of Emperor Qian Long, inscribed the eulogy of 2,000 characters on the stone tablets in Manchu and Chinese languages.

牌楼门 位于石像生北,五间六柱五楼,属点缀建筑,系景陵首创。图为裕陵牌楼门。

Archway Tower The archway tower to the north of the stone sculptures at Dingling has five openings separated by six pillars. The first archway in the form of a tower was built at Jingling.

焚帛炉 又名燎炉,位于隆恩门北,通体由琉璃件构成,晶莹剔透,小巧玲珑,是祭祀结束后烧化祝版、制帛和金银锞子的地方。帝后陵设两座,妃园寝仅一座。

Sacrificial Silk Burners Located to the north of Long'en Gate, the burners are exquisitely built of glazed pottery. After a sacrificial ceremony the prayer paper, paper-made gold and silver ingots were burned in them. The emperor's tomb has two such burners, but the imperial concubine's tomb has only one.

乾隆御制诗雕刻匾 是乾隆皇帝为悼念其原配皇后富察氏(1712－1748年)而作。富察氏于乾隆十三年崩于德州，乾隆皇帝十分悲痛，谥孝贤皇后，于乾隆十七年入葬东陵。以后谒陵，乾隆皇帝曾多次赋诗哀悼。这些诗被制成雕漆匾，陈列在裕陵隆恩殿内。图中匾上所刻诗作于癸未年，即乾隆二十八年。

Emperor Qian Long's Poetry Boards   Emperor Qian Long wrote these poems in memory of his first wife Fucha (1712-1748). After Fucha died in Dezhou, the emperor grieved over her death and posthumously entitled her Empress Xiao Xian. Her remains were moved from Dezhou and buried in this cemetery. Later, when the emperor went to visit her tomb, he wrote poems in memory of her. These poems were inscribed on lacquer boards and placed in the Long'en Hall of Yuling. The poem in the picture was written in the 28th year of the Qian Long Reign.

裕陵玉带桥 玉带桥三座并排，长仅三米，宽不足二米，以纤巧取胜。在隆恩殿后河道上建拱形玉带桥，在清帝陵中仅此一例。

Jade-Belt Bridge of Yuling   Three bridges stand together. Exquisitely constructed, they are only three metres long and less than two metres wide each. Only the Yuling tomb has such bridges over the river behind the Long'en Hall in the Qing tombs.

二柱门 立于陵寝门与石五供之间,双柱抱楼,柱顶二只蹲龙相向而视。楼顶覆黄瓦,梁枋绘烟琢墨石碾玉旋子彩画。二柱门起着后寝部分影壁墙的作用,它隔绝着"天国"与"尘世",使人世的纷扰与喧嚣远离仙逝的帝后们所居住的"天堂"——地宫。

Twin-Pillar Gate The gate, standing between the Memorial Hall and the Stone Altar Pieces, is supported by two stone pillars. The dragons on top of the pillars gaze at each other. With a yellow glazed tile roof, the gate is beautifully painted. It plays the role of a wall screen to separate "heaven" from "the earthly world" so that noise from the human world would not disturb the dead in the underground palace.

方城明楼 方城在宝城之前,以其为方形而得名,上建明楼。清帝陵的方城,加大了基座的高度,在石五供的衬托下,更显高大巍峨,使人顿生"景行景止,高山仰止"之情思。

Square City and Memorial Tower The square city lies just before the tomb mound and the memorial tower stands on top of the square city. The square cities of the Qing emperors' tombs have a higher wall and look more magnificent when they are set off by the Stone Altar Pieces.

地宫 位于宝顶下面，是安放棺椁的地方。图为裕陵地宫，其壮观与豪华为清陵所有已开放地宫之最。它由九券四门组成，券顶、券壁和石门上满刻佛教题材的图案，堪称地下佛堂。

Underground Palace　The picture shows the burial chamber of Yuling. It is the most complex and lavishly decorated burial chamber of the Qing tombs so far excavated, consisting of nine vaults and four gates. On the arched ceilings, walls and gates are relief carvings describing Buddhist images.

文殊菩萨 地宫内八扇石门上，各刻一尊生动的菩萨立像。图中文殊菩萨雕在第一道石门东扇上，她头顶莲花佛冠，身披缨络菊花，赤脚立于出水芙蓉之上。雕刻细腻，线条流畅，具有较高的艺术价值。

Relief Caving of Manjusri On each of the eight doors in the Underground Palace is carved the image of a standing Bodhisattva. The picture shows the image of Manjusri on the eastern door of the first gate. Wearing a lotus flower crown and a robe laced with pearls, it stands on a water lily blossom barefooted. The carving of excellent craftsmanship is of high artistic value.

地宫石门 裕陵地宫石门均由整块青白石制成,高3米、宽1.5米、厚0.19米,重约三吨,门上巧妙地安装了一根重一万多斤的方形整体铜管扇,使沉重的石门运转自如。每道石门内用一根"自来石"顶住,使石门从外面难以打开。图为第二道石门。

Stone Doors of the Underground Palace The doors of the Yuling Underground Palace are three metres high, 1.5 metres wide and 0.19 metre thick and weigh about three tons each. They are carved out of a whole piece of white marble. Fixed on a whole square bronze leaf of more than ten thousand *jin*, the heavy stone doors can move freely. Once they are shut and locked with a stone rod from inside, it is difficult to open them from outside. The picture shows the stone doors of the second gate.

持国天王 地宫第一道门洞券里雕刻着四大天王像，图为持国天王，他以琵琶为法器，守护着佛经中须弥山的东方。

Relief Carving of Dhrtarastra
Carved on the wall of the first entrance to the burial chamber are the images of the Four Deva-Kings. The picture shows Dhrtarastra holding a *pipa* lute as a weapon. He is the guardian of the eastern part of the world.

穿堂券顶佛像 第二道石门内的穿堂券券顶刻 24 尊佛像，各结不同姿势的手印。佛像间饰火珠、法轮、宝杵、莲花等佛教法物，宝像庄严，仪态万方。每座佛像身后，都有形似龛座的"背光"，以花卉为装饰，图案丰富细腻。

Buddhist Images on the Arched Ceiling On the arched ceiling of the passage inside the second gate are carved 24 images of Buddha in different postures with balls of fire, wheels of the law and lotus flowers between them. Behind the images is the "back light" of the shrine with flower and plant motif. The carving is of excellent craftsmanship.

狮子进宝 狮子在中国被视为百兽之王。裕陵地宫雕刻的这头雄狮，背驮宝瓶进贡，寓意皇家威震天下，统摄四方。

Lion Presents Treasure In China the lion is regarded as the king of animals. This stone lion in the burial chamber of Yuling carries a precious bottle to the dead emperor, meaning that the royal power was the highest.

五欲供 刻于第三道石门内穿堂券的东西两壁。五朵莲花分别托起明镜、琵琶、涂香、水果、天衣五种器物，暗喻人类对"色、声、香、味、触"的欲望，告诫人们破除五欲，才能修成正果。构思机智，借喻巧妙。

Carvings about Sensual Desires These carvings are on the eastern and western walls of the passage inside the third stone gate. In the five vases are lotus flowers, on top of which are mirror, *pipa* lute, powder, fruit and heavenly robe to suggest sensual desires. It shows that only those who rid themselves of sensual desires can have their soul released from purgatory.

地宫金券　为地宫最主要部分,是安放帝后梓宫之处。内设宝床,上置乾隆皇帝和五位后妃的棺椁。1928 年孙殿英盗陵,棺椁被毁,随葬品亦被洗劫一空。

Burial Chamber　This is the main part of the underground palace of Yuling. It holds the coffins of Emperor Qian Long and his five consorts. In 1928 Warlord Sun Dianying plundered Yuling and destroyed the coffins.

妃园寝 即清代妃嫔的墓葬群。图为裕陵妃园寝,位于裕陵西,内葬乾隆皇帝的 36 位后妃。裕妃园寝设东西配殿,建方城明楼,超越了规制。

Tombs of Imperial Concubines During the reign of Emperor Kang Xi, special grounds were set aside for imperial concubines in the imperial cemeteries. The picture shows the tomb of the imperial concubine at Yuling, which contains the remains of 36 concubines of Emperor Qian Long. The tomb has two wing halls and a front hall, an addition to the tomb exceeding the status of imperial concubines.

焚帛炉 其结构形式与帝后陵焚帛炉相同，但规制低，故其琉璃瓦构件用绿色，且只在东侧设一座。

Sacrificial Silk Burner This burner lying on the eastern side of the tomb of imperial concubines is the same in structure as that at the tombs of emperors and empresses. But the tombs of emperors and empresses have two such burners constructed of yellow glazed pottery, and the tombs of imperial concubines have only one made of green glazed pottery.

纯惠皇贵妃地宫 为皇贵妃地宫之典型,计有五券一门。金券内石床正中为纯惠皇贵妃棺椁,其左停放那拉皇后棺椁。那拉皇后于乾隆三十年(1765年)随帝南巡时惹恼了皇帝,从此失宠,死后仅以皇贵妃礼葬入妃园寝,未建单独的宝顶地宫,且棺椁摆在卑位,尚不如一般妃嫔。

Burial Chamber of Lady Chunhui The burial chamber is composed of five arched vaults and one gate. The coffin of Lady Chunhui is placed on a stone platform in the last vault. In its right is the coffin of Empress Nala. Empress Nala lost the favour of Emperor Qian Long and was buried with an imperial concubine when she died. There is no separate earth mound for her above the ground.

◀ **宝顶群** 裕妃园寝后院,顺序排列35个宝顶,其下埋葬着乾隆皇帝的36位后妃。宝顶位置先后、规模大小皆显示出墓主生前地位的尊卑。

Earth Mounds Under the 35 earth mounds in the backyard of the imperial concubine tome are the remains of 36 imperial concubines of Emperor Qian Long. The mounds vary in height and size according to the status of the dead lying beneath them.

香妃　是一位富有传奇色彩的女子，相传她是新疆回部小和卓木霍集占的妃子，不假熏沐而体有异香，清军平定回疆后被俘，誓死不从乾隆皇帝，被太后赐死，归葬新疆。实际上，香妃即乾隆皇帝的容妃，她的家庭在清军平定回疆中立有大功，为国家的统一和民族团结做出了贡献。

Burial Chamber of Lady Xiangfei　According to legend, Xiangfei was the concubine of a local ruler in Xinjiang and emitted a nice scent from her body without applying perfume. She was captured after the Qing troops took Xinjiang. Emperor Qian Long wanted to make her his concubine, but she preferred to die rather than agree. Finally the emperor's mother bestowed death on her, and her body was buried in Xinjiang. In fact Xiangfei was Emperor Qian Long's Concubine Rongfei. Her family contributed to the unification of the country and to the unity of all nationalities.

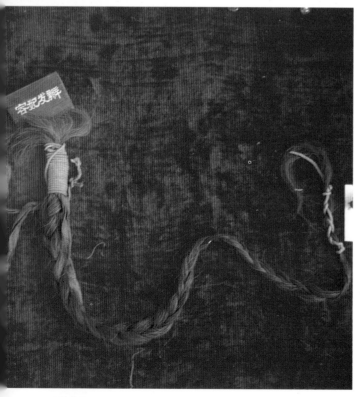

容妃发辫　容妃于乾隆二十五年二月入宫，时年27岁，封为和贵人，后来累晋为容妃。于乾隆五十三年四月病死于宫中，时年55岁。地宫中这条发辫，颜色灰白，更加证实了她非年轻时被太后赐死，而系年老善终。

Rongfei's Hair　Rongfei was sent to the imperial palace when she was 27 in the 25th year of the Qian Long Reign and died at the age of 55 in the 53rd year of the Qian Long Reign. The grey hair in the burial chamber verifies that she was not killed young on the order of the emperor's mother but died a natural death.

容妃地宫 为清代典型的妃型地宫,计有四券一门。其棺椁上有手书的阿拉伯文《古兰经》金字,是死者生前信仰及民族所属的证物。

Burial Chamber of Rongfei This is a typical burial chamber for an imperial concubine with four vaults and one gate. On the coffin was inscribed the Koran in gold, which shows the belief and nationality of the deceased.

定陵远眺 定陵是清朝入关后第七位皇帝咸丰皇帝的陵寝,其建筑规制承前启后,既遵守祖宗成宪,又部分采用清西陵慕陵慕陵的做法,如裁去圣德神功碑亭、二柱门等,再加上自己的创新,形成了独特的建筑布局,开创了新的陵寝修建规制。

Dingling Viewed from the Distance This is the tomb of Emperor Xian Feng, the 7th emperor of the Qing after the Manchus established their regime in Beijing. The buildings are arranged in a new and compact layout. Some buildings such as the Stele Pavilion and Twin-Pillar Gate are omitted.

定陵石望柱 位于石像生南端，柱身遍刻舒卷自如的祥云，在蓝天白云和苍松翠柏的映衬下，亭亭玉立，丰姿绰约。

Stone Column of Dingling Located at the southern end of the Stone Sculptures, the stone column is exquisitely carved in auspicious clouds motif. It stands erect among green pine and cypress trees beneath the blue sky with drifting white clouds.

咸丰皇帝画像 咸丰皇帝(1851－1861年在位),名爱新觉罗.奕詝,年号咸丰,庙号文宗。他即位伊始就爆发了声势浩大的太平天国农民运动。1856年,英法联军又发动了第二次鸦片战争。1861年,在内忧外患中死于避暑山庄,一生无大作为。

Portrait of Emperor Xian Feng Emperor Xian Feng was on the throne from 1851 to 1861. Just after he was enthroned, the great Taiping Peasant Uprising took place, and in 1856 the Second Opium War broke out. He died in 1861 at the Summer Resort in Chengde at a time when the country was beset by domestic trouble and foreign invasion.

定陵牌楼门 定陵地势陡峭,故沿路设置了三重泊岸,使得陵寝建筑物层层叠叠,渐次升高。从牌楼门北望,神道碑亭、东朝房等建筑参差错落,并然有序。

Archway Tower of Dingling As the tomb is situated on a steep mountainside, the buildings rise one higher than the other. Viewed from the archway tower, the buildings such as the Stele Pavilion along the Sacred Way come into sight.

省牲亭　位于神厨库院内东南角,为宰杀祭祀用牛羊之处。内设锅灶及厨房用具等。

Slaughterhouse　It is located in the southeastern corner in the compound of the Offerings Kitchen. Cattle and sheep were killed here for sacrifice.

神厨库　是帝后陵的附属建筑物,位于神道碑亭以东,红墙环绕,自成一院,院内迎门有神厨五间,是制作肉食祭品的地方。南北各三间为神库,是存放神厨祭品及原料之处。

Offerings Kitchen　It is located to the east of the Stele Pavilion on the Sacred Way and surrounded by a red wall. The kitchen was used to cook the meat for sacrificial ceremony. To its south and north there are storehouses for keeping tools and raw materials.

东配殿 位于焚帛炉北,是存放祭祀用祝版、制帛的殿堂。逢隆恩殿大修,亦临时存放墓主牌位。图为定陵东配殿。

Eastern Wing Hall
The hall to the north of the sacrificial paper burner served as a storehouse for sacrificial papers. When the main memorial hall was under repair, memorial tablets with the titles of the deceased emperor were moved here. The picture shows the Eastern Wing Hall of Dingling.

定陵隆恩殿 隆恩殿东、西、北三面不设栏板、栏柱,造型结构,别具一格。

Long'en Hall of Dingling This hall was modelled after Muling in the Western Qing Tombs. It has no surrounding corridor, no balustrade on the three sides of the east, west and north. The design is very special.

隆恩殿内景 清陵以清明、中元(即七月十五日)、冬至、岁暮、帝后忌辰为五大祭,多由王公致祭,有时皇帝也亲临主持。图中表现的是同治十二年(1873年)皇帝主持大祭礼的情景。持香行礼者为同治皇帝。

Inside the Long'en Hall Five grand sacrificial ceremonies were held at the imperial cemetery in a year. Most of them were presided over by princes. The living emperor appeared only occasionally. The picture depicts Emperor Tong Zhi at a sacrificial ceremony held in 1873.

五供基座雕刻 五供基座为须弥座,上枋雕缠枝西番莲,下枋雕暗八仙、八宝,寓意众神将最珍贵最灵验的礼物奉献给皇帝。

Altar-Piece Dais Five altar-pieces are placed on a stone dais carved with flower designs on the upper part and on the lower part the Eight Immortals, each holding a precious present for the deceased emperor.

明楼 定陵地势陡峭,从五供仰视明楼,愈显气势雄浑。

Memorial Tower of Dingling　The tower rises high above the front gate of the wall surrounding the earth mound at Dingling.

明楼翼角彩画 明楼黄瓦飞甍,梁枋、斗栱、椽飞上饰烟琢墨石碾玉彩画,檐椽头上描龙眼宝珠,飞椽头上绘金井玉栏杆。墨、绿、白三色相映,艳丽高雅。

Painted Eaves of the Memorial Tower The rafters of the tower are painted with spirals and the brackets with red and green motifs. It is extremely colourful.

月牙城 为方城和宝城之间的一进院落,因其四面被砖墙包围,形似月牙,故名月牙城,为帝陵所特有。其北墙正中琉璃影壁处是地宫入口,传说为防止泄密,雇用哑巴在此施工,故俗称哑巴院。

Crescent Castle It is a courtyard in the shape of a crescent moon inside the wall and in front of the earth mound. A screen wall of glazed tiles is the beginning of a tunnel to the underground burial chamber. The builders of the courtyard were mutes who could not tell the secrets of the tomb. So the courtyard is also called "Mutes' Yard".

七星沟漏　设于月牙城地面的渗水孔。工匠们在地面安设七星沟漏，将积水汇于地下通道排往玉带河，以保持陵院干燥，构思可谓精巧。

Seven-Star Water Gargoyle　Rain water drains through seven holes in marble blocks at the ground level in the courtyard of the tomb into the Jade-Belt River. It is a well-designed drainage system.

玉带河　位于石五供和明楼之间，用于排泄陵寝宝城后院及哑巴院内的积水。其河道东高西低，积水向西排出陵院外，为防止外人从出水口进入陵内，院墙出口处有粗大的铸铁箅条。

Jade-Belt River　The river lies between the Five Altar-Pieces and the Memorial Tower. Rain water inside the Precious City and Mutes' Yard is drained through it. To prevent people from entering the tomb through the river, iron bars are set at its outlet.

宝顶 即坟堆,其下为安放棺椁的地宫。定陵宝顶改变了传统做法。以前各帝陵金券券顶上覆琉璃瓦,定陵则用糙新样城砖灌浆垒砌成庑殿蓑衣顶,然后用三合土夯成长圆形宝顶。

"**Precious Top**" This is tomb mound. Beneath it is the underground palace where the emperor's coffin is placed. Tombs of earlier Qing emperors had an arched roof. Dingling began to have a gabled and hipped roof over the burial chamber. After the underground chamber was finished, a mixture of earth and lime was piled on the roof to form a mound, which was called "Precious Top".

挡水坝 即陵寝北面罗圈墙外两段弧形大理石墙。定陵山势险峻,陵寝易受山洪冲刷,挡水坝将山洪截住,使之向两侧分流,保护了陵寝的安全。

Water Dam Two semicircular walls stand on each side of the tomb to block off and divert any runoff of rain water from the mountainside behind the tomb.

定东陵 是咸丰皇帝两位皇后慈安和慈禧的陵寝,因其位于定陵之东,故名。两陵间仅隔一条马槽沟,建筑规制和修建年代完全相同。从后山俯瞰定东陵,建筑物重重叠叠,鳞次栉比,美不胜收。

Eastern Dingling This mausoleum is composed of two tombs, one for Ci An and one for Ci Xi, two empresses of Emperor Xian Feng. They were of the same plan, separated by a ditch. Their construction was begun in the same year. It provides a magnificent scene when viewed from the mountain behind the mausoleum.

慈禧太后画像 慈禧太后(1835－1908 年)，叶赫那拉氏，咸丰二年入宫，初号兰贵人，同治帝生母。1861 年与慈安太后勾结恭亲王奕訢发动北京政变后垂帘听政，执掌朝政达 48 年之久，是中国近代史上的传奇人物。

Portrait of Empress Dowager Ci Xi Ci Xi (1835-1908), a concubine of Xian Feng, the seventh emperor of the Qing Dynasty. In 1861, after the emperor died, she collaborated with Empress Ci An and Prince Gong for a coup d'etat and took power to "rule behind the curtain" for 48 years. She is a legendary figure in Chinese history.

慈禧陵隆恩殿　慈禧陵和慈安陵的初建规制完全相同，但光绪二十一年(1895年)，慈禧太后以年久失修为由，令重修其陵。重建后的隆恩殿和东西配殿，梁枋全部改用名贵的黄花梨木，内壁改成砖雕图案，外墙磨砖到顶，内外装修极为豪华。

Long'en Hall of Ci Xi's Tomb　Ci Xi's tomb was constructed of the same plan as that of Ci An. But in 1895 Ci Xi ordered her tomb rebuilt on the pretext that it was in disrepair. The beams, rafters and windows of the Long'en Hall of the reconstructed tomb are made of precious pear wood. The inside walls are covered with brick carvings and the outside ones are built of highly-polished bricks.

慈禧陵金龙柱 重修后的慈禧陵三殿内外 64 根柱子上均饰有一条铜鎏金半立体蟠龙,龙须以弹簧制成,借助空气流通,须髯自然摆动,如群龙低吟,令人叹为观止。图为 20 年代三殿外景。

Pillars with Coiled Dragons Each of the 64 pillars inside the Sandian Hall at Ci Xi's tomb is decorated with a relief coiled dragon of gilded bronze. The dragon's beard is made of springs, which waves in the wind and produces sounds like the groans of many dragons. The picture is an outside scene of the Sandian Hall in the 1920s.

丹陛石 放置在隆恩殿前,采用高浮雕加透雕的工艺,增强了立体感。它一改龙凤并排的丹陛惯例为凤上龙下,反映了当时皇太后垂帘听政的政治形势。 ▶

Stone Block The stone block lies in front of the Long'en Hall. It is carved in relief and hollow, giving a three-dimensional impression. The relief caving has a dragon and a phoenix. Against the long tradition which puts the dragon above the phoenix, the design at Ci Xi's tomb has the phoenix riding above the dragon. It shows the political situation that Empress Dowager Ci Xi was manipulating state affairs from "behind the curtain" at that time. ▶

石雕 隆恩殿周围的汉白玉石望柱打破了历来一龙一凤相间的"龙凤望柱"格式,柱头全部雕刻凤凰,柱身为两条仰望的升龙。栏板上雕69幅龙凤呈祥、水浪浮云图案,彩凤在前展翅飞翔,蛟龙在后振爪奋追,其情其景是同治、光绪两朝慈禧太后专权的艺术再现。

Stone Carvings Relief carvings on the marble balusters around Long'en Hall depict 69 pairs of dragon and phoenix playing amidst water waves and clouds. The phoenix surges ahead of the dragon, symbolizing Empress Dowager Ci Xi leading the country during the reigns of Emperor Tong Zhi and Emperor Guang Xu.

螭首 传为龙子之一,又名苍龙头,安置在隆恩殿四角和月台两角。慈禧陵的螭首,卷鼻突目,翘首苍穹,气度不凡。

Chi's **Head** According to Chinese mythology, *chi* is one of the nine sons of the dragon. It loves water, so its image is often seen at a water outlet. At Ci Xi's tomb, *chi* is placed at the four corners of Long'en Hall and on both sides of the platform with a raised head and a protruded nose.

铜鹿　置于隆恩殿月台上，清帝陵设铜鹿、铜鹤各一对；自泰东陵始，皇后陵各设一只。月台上设鹿鹤，取其谐音，寓"六合同春"之意。

Bronze Deer　It is placed at the platform in front of Long'en Hall. Emperor's tombs of the Qing Dynasty have a pair of bronze deer and a pair of bronze cranes in front of their main halls, but the empress' tombs have only one bronze deer and one bronze crane, symbolizing peace and prosperity.

万福流云图　慈禧陵隆恩殿墙体上方周围的拔檐上，刻"卐"字、蝙蝠和流云图案。表达了人们祈求幸福的美好愿望。图案雕刻细腻，精巧奇特，不愧艺术珍品。

Various Patterns　The upper walls and the eaves of Long'en Hall at Ci Xi's tomb are carved in relief with various auspicious patterns such as "Five Bats at Birthday Celebration" and continuous links of the symbol for longevity. These carvings have high artistic value.

隆恩殿内景 内塑慈禧太后扮观音像。慈禧太后性格暴戾，但笃信佛教。她曾数次扮成观音，头戴毗卢帽，端坐于莲花台上，左侧李莲英扮做韦驮尊者，右侧为一面庞姣丽的少女扮龙女。前为荷花丛，后为紫竹林。蜡像所塑人物栩栩如生。

Inside Long'en Hall This waxwork in Long'en Hall shows how Empress Dowager Ci Xi dressed up as Quanyin (Goddess of Mercy) in a Buddhist crown and robe and holding a string of beads. She sits on a lotus flower seat. Her favourite eunuch Li Lianying stands on her left and a beautiful young girl stands on her right. In front of her is a cluster of lotus flowers and behind her is a cluster of bamboo.

金龙柱 几十年战乱，慈禧陵三殿的金龙未存一鳞半爪，只是那残留的殿柱上还依稀可见金龙盘玉柱的痕迹。为了再现那举世奇迹，清东陵管理处拨巨款恢复了殿内四条金龙柱。跨入殿内，但见那金龙张牙舞爪，令人惊羡。

Pillars with Coiled Golden Dragons The golden dragons coiled on the pillars in the hall at Ci Xi's tomb were destroyed in wars in the past. Only their traces were left on the pillars. To show what those dragons were like, the Management Office of the Eastern Qing Tombs restored them. Baring fangs and brandishing claws, these dragons are quite awesome.

"五福捧寿"砖雕　慈禧陵三殿内壁上,有八幅
"五福捧寿"砖雕图案,图案中心有团"寿"字,外
绕两环,大环外五只蝙蝠,头朝寿字,展翅飞翔。
图案构思精巧,借助谐音手法,揭示出"五福捧
寿"的主题。五福语出《尚书》,指寿、富、康宁、
攸好德、考终命五种吉祥之事。

"Five Bats at Birthday Celebration" Brick Carvings
On the inside walls of the hall at Ci Xi's tomb are
eight brick carvings in the pattern of "Five Bats at
Birthday Celebration". In the centre of the carvings is the word "Longevity" encircled by five fly-
ing bats with their heads ingeniously turned to the
word "Longevity".

"万字不到头"砖雕 在"五福捧寿"图案外有一方形掐珠子圈框,四角各刻一组"盘长",正中串一条轻柔飘舞的绶带,底为"卐"字不到头雕刻。寄托"江山万代,福寿绵长"之意。慈禧陵内壁砖雕,用筛扫黄金手法装饰,与彩画交相辉映,浑然一体。

"卐" Brick Carvings Outside the "Five Bats at Birthday Celebration" carvings is a square formed by beads. At each of the four corners of the square is a linked symbol with a ribbon floating through it. Beneath the linked symbol is the pattern "卐". The carvings symbolize "Qing power lasts for ten thousand generations and its rulers live on for ever". The brick carvings form an integral whole with the paintings in the hall at Ci Xi's tomb.

天花板图案 慈禧陵天花板所绘图案亦与其他帝后陵不同,不施彩绘,而是用金箔贴绘成正龙形象,外围饰云纹。龙是皇帝的象征,一般不单独绘于皇后陵,这也是慈禧陵逾制的地方。可惜这些珍贵的文物已多被盗走,现仅存四块半。

Decorations on the Ceilings Decorations on the ceilings of the hall at Ci Xi's tomb are also different from other Qing tombs. They are not painted but pasted in gold foil in the form of the dragon amidst clouds. Dragon symbolized the emperor and was not applicable to the empress. But Empress Dowager Ci Xi used it. Unfortunately, most of the decorations were stolen. Only four and half pieces are left today.

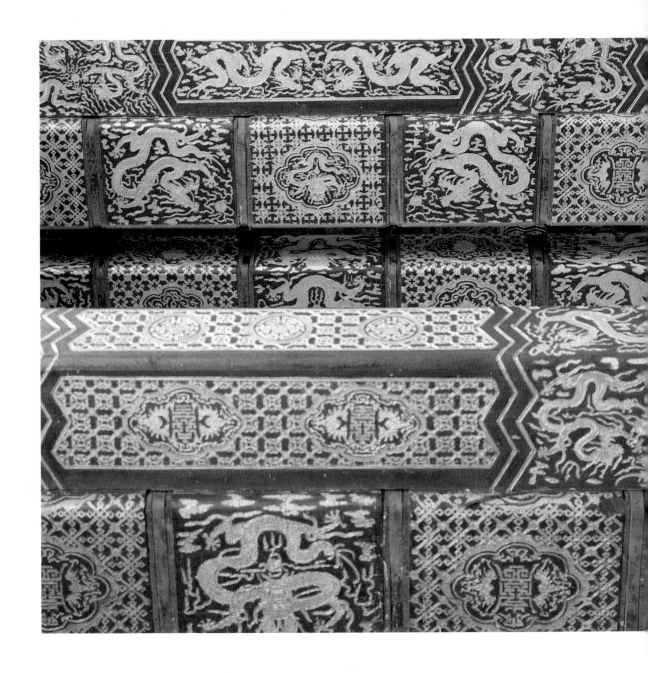

金龙和玺彩画　清陵建筑多饰旋子彩画,唯慈禧陵三殿绘等级最高的金龙和玺彩画。彩画用金箔镶贴出二龙戏珠、寿字等不同图案,线条繁密细腻,风格典雅华美,表现了清代彩画的高超技艺。图为西配殿内彩画。

Decorative Motifs　Most of buildings in the Qing tombs bear decorative motifs of spirals on pillars, beams and windows. But the motifs on the hall at Ci Xi's tomb are two dragons playing with a pearl or in the shape of the Chinese character for longevity. The picture shows the painted motifs inside Long'en Hall.

金漆木塔 用于保留慈禧太后生前剪下的指甲和梳掉的头发。中国古人认为"身之发肤,受之父母,不可毁伤。"生前要妥贴保管,死后要纳于棺,慈禧太后棺椁内就有指甲一包。

Gilt Lacquered Wooden Pagoda This wooden pagoda is the container Empress Dowager Ci Xi used to hold her nails and hair. Ancient Chinese believed that "the hair and skin of the body come from the parents and can't be thrown away", and they must be kept when one was alive and buried together with the body in the coffin when one died. Inside Ci Xi's coffin there is a bag of her nails.

神牌 用于供奉的写着死者谥号的金漆木牌。图为慈禧太后神牌,其上用满、蒙、汉三种文字刻着慈禧太后的谥号。平时,神牌供放在隆恩殿暖阁的宝床上,每逢大祭,由礼部官员从暖阁内请出,置于宝座上受享。

Memorial Tablet The memorial tablet is a gilt lacquered wood board, on which was inscribed the title of the deceased. The picture shows Empress Dowager Ci Xi's memorial tablet with her title inscribed on it in Manchu, Mongolian and Chinese languages. In ordinary times it was kept in the Warm Chamber in Long'en Hall, and when a sacrificial ceremony was held, it was placed on the chair behind the sacrificial table.

三座门　又名陵寝门，位于隆恩殿后。慈禧陵的三座门，中门和左右角门均装饰中心花和岔角花，为清帝后陵所独有。

Three-Door Entrance Also called the tomb gate, it lies behind the Long'en Hall. The Three-Door Entrance to Ci Xi's tomb has beautiful decorations on the three doors. Only the tombs of Qing emperors and empresses have such entrance.

石五供 位于方城前,为象征性祭器。五供指鼎炉一座、烛台一对、花瓶一对。图为慈禧陵石五供,雕刻手法细腻,风格独特,堪为石雕艺术珍品。

Five Altar-Pieces The five stone altar-pieces placed in front of the Square City are symbolic sacrificial objects including an incense burner, a pair of candlesticks and a pair of flower vases. These in the picture are placed at Ci Xi's tomb. The relief sculpture is of high craftsmanship.

慈禧太后地宫　典型的后陵地宫,五券二门,雕刻华美,选料精良。陵院有完整的排水系统,建筑设计更趋合理。

Burial Chamber for Empress Dowager Ci Xi　The chamber is built with fine materials and composed of five vaults and two gates with fine relief carvings. The tomb is kept dry with a perfect drainage system.

慈禧太后棺椁　用金丝楠木制成,分内棺、外椁两部分。清制,帝后棺椁髹漆 49 道,外涂金漆,内棺刻佛经,红漆填金。1928 年,孙殿英盗陵,慈禧太后尸骨被抛出棺外,后经考古人员整理放于棺内。

Coffins of Empress Dowager Ci Xi　The remains of Empress Dowager Ci Xi are placed in two coffins one inside the other. Made of precious *nanmu* wood, the coffins were painted with 49 layers of lacquer. The outermost coating was mixed with gold powder and the inside coffin was inscribed with Buddhist scriptures. In 1928 warlord Sun Dianying blew open the tomb to loot the treasures inside. The remains of Ci Xi were scattered. Later, archaeologists collected the remains and put them back in the coffin.

慈禧陵盗口 慈禧太后陵亦于 1928 年被孙殿英部盗掘,随后逊清皇室会同南京政府派员对被盗陵寝进行勘察,对两陵地宫内葬人物重新装殓。图为各界人员和军警勘察地宫时的情景。

The Hole Left by the Plunderers After Empress Dowager Ci Xi's tomb was plundered by Sun Dianying's troops in 1928, the abdicated Qing royal family and the Nanjing government made an investigation of the plundered tombs and re-dressed and put the corpses back to the coffins. The picture shows people and police investigating the underground palace then.

香宝 帝后入葬时,以檀香木制的香册和香宝(印)随葬地宫,册宝置于箱中,放在第一道石门内的石制册宝座上。图为慈禧太后香宝,其上用满、汉两种文字阳刻慈禧太后的全部谥号。宝文为古篆字,诘屈蟠曲,古拙典雅。

Fragrant Treasures When emperors and empresses were buried, these "Fragrant Treasures" — the Register and Seal made of sandalwood — were buried together with them in the underground palace. They were put in a box and placed on a stone table inside the first stone gate. The picture shows Empress Dowager Ci Xi's Seal inscribed with her title in Manchu and Chinese languages.

纱袍 为慈禧太后夏装,制作者在淡褐纱地上平织竹叶,中间夹杂用金线织成的团寿字。慈禧太后十分喜欢此袍,69 岁大寿时曾穿着照相留念,现在慈禧陵内展出。

Gauze Robe The summer wear of Empress Dowager Ci Xi is inlaid with patterns of bamboo leaves and the Chinese character for longevity of gold filaments. Ci Xi posed for a picture in it on her 69th birthday. The robe is displayed at Ci Xi's tomb.

祭器 帝后陵寝祭祀时,要使用种类繁多的祭器。祭器的瓷器中,有椭圆形的簋、长方形的簠,圆形带耳的铏,顶上带圆钮的豆及酒爵、羊耳大尊等。

Sacrificial Objects When sacrificial ceremonies were held, various objects were used. Most of them were made of porcelain in different shapes and sizes.

饰物　为慈禧陵展品,有香囊、香排、手串等。中国自古就有佩香草的习俗,香草被视为君子的象征,后来发展为"香囊",有佩之以自我砥励的意思。香排的作用亦同。

Ornaments　Displayed on the exhibition at Ci Xi's tomb is a magnitude of ornamental articles including strings of pearls, perfume bags and embroidered pouches. There was the custom of wearing sweetgrass in China in ancient times. Sweetgrass became the symbol of gentlemen. Later perfume bags appeared. They emitted a pleasant scent.

珐琅荷叶瓶与太平有象 慈禧陵展品。珐琅荷叶瓶,铜胎外填珐琅釉,瓶腹为绿色荷叶,肩上填莲蓬,瓶耳为两截莲藕,有浓郁的水乡生活气息。太平有象,典型的宫廷题材,寓意国泰民安。

Enamel Lotus-Leave Vase and Elephant These articles are exhibited at Ci Xi's tomb. The vase has a bronze roughcast coated in enamel. Inside it is a green lotus leave. On top of it are lotuses. Its two handles are in shape of lotus roots. The elephant is the symbol of peace and prosperity.

象牙雕笔筒、瓜、小盒 慈安陵展品。笔筒上透雕亭台楼阁、水榭轩亭和人物,细致入微,丝丝入扣,有较高的欣赏价值。香瓜形态逼真,瓜蔓盘曲,瓜叶上的纹路,清晰可见,既有文物价值,又是一件不可多得的艺术品。

Ivory Brush Pot, Melon and Small Box These also are exhibits at Ci An's tomb. The ivory brush pot is exquisitely carved with towers, pavilions and figures. The melon is very lifelike. They are of high artistic value.

惠陵全景　清朝入关后第八位皇帝同治帝(1862－1874 年在位)之陵。始建于光绪元年(1875 年)，历时三年完工，是清朝各帝陵中施工期最短的陵寝。惠陵裁撤了通往孝陵的神路和石像生、圣德神功碑亭、二柱门等建筑，在东陵诸帝陵中最朴。但其梁架所用梓檀木坚硬无比，有"铜梁铁柱"之称。

Huiling It is the tomb of Emperor Tong Zhi (reigned 1862-74), the eighth emperor of the Qing Dynasty after the Manchus established their regime in Beijing. Construction began in 1875 and was finished in three years, the shortest construction time of the Qing tombs. The tomb does not have the usual Sacred Way to connect it with the main tomb of Xiaoling, the Stone Sculptures, the Divine Merit Stele Tower or the Twin-Pillar Gate. It is the simplest of the Eastern Qing Tombs. The pillars and beams of the halls are made of hard sandalwood and known as "Bronze Pillars and Iron Beams".

神道碑 位于神道碑亭正中，又称"庙号碑"，其上用满、蒙、汉三种文字刻着墓主的庙号和谥号。图为惠陵神道碑。

Stele on the Sacred Way The stele at the centre of the pavilion is inscribed in Manchu, Mongolian and Chinese languages with the title of the emperor buried in the tomb. The stele in the picture belongs to Huiling.

明楼石碑 位于明楼正中,碑趺为须弥座,上竖"朱砂碑"一统,碑身正面用满、蒙、汉三种文字刻着"穆宗毅皇帝之陵"七个贴金大字。

Stele in the Memorial Tower The stele stands on a stone base in the centre of the tower. On it is written "Tomb of Emperor Mu Zong Yi" covered in gold leaf.

惠陵明楼 从陵寝中门仰视明楼,青砖红墙黄瓦彩画,尽纳方形景框中,美不胜收。

Memorial Tower of Huiling The tower has a grey brick base, red walls and a yellow tile roof with exquisitely painted eaves. It gives beautiful sight when viewed from the entrance.

孝庄文皇后朝服像 孝庄文皇后，博尔济吉特氏，为清太宗永福宫庄妃，因所生皇九子福临即位为皇帝，尊为皇太后。她曾先后辅佐顺治、康熙两代幼主开基创业，是清初的传奇性人物。"太后下嫁"（孝庄文皇后下嫁摄政王多尔衮）成为清初三大疑案之一。

Portrait of Empress Xiaozhuang Wen in Her Ceremonial Clothes Empress Xiaozhuang Wen became an empress dowager after her ninth son Fu Lin was made emperor. The capable empress helped two young emperors (one her son, the other her grandson) consolidate their power. She is a legendary figure of the early Qing Dynasty.

昭西陵 孝庄文皇后的陵寝。康熙二十七年(1688年)始建,初名为"暂安奉殿",雍正三年(1725年)改建成皇后陵。从地理位置看,此陵位于沈阳皇太极的昭陵之西,故名。昭西陵建筑规模较大,陵垣为二重,隆恩殿为重檐庑殿式,建下马碑、神道碑亭,在皇后陵中规制最高。

Western Zhaoling　It is the tomb of Empress Xiao-zhuang Wen. It was first built in the 27th year of the Kang Xi Reign (1688) and later reconstructed into an empress' tomb in the third year of the Yong Zheng Reign (1725). The tomb is located to the west of Zhaoling in Shenyang city, so it is called Western Zhaoling. In a large scale, the tomb has two surrounding walls, a double-eave Long'en Hall, a stele for officials to dismount from horseback, and a stele tower on the Sacred Way. It is the largest of the empress' tombs.

二郎庙全景 二郎庙是东陵陵区内唯一的庙宇。清朝始建东陵时，命将陵区内所有庙宇一概迁出，但考虑到二郎庙前有座名叫"猴山"的小山，为了镇住"闹事"的猴子，遂将此庙留下。今庙宇正殿内除供奉主神二郎外，还有八仙中的吕洞宾(798－? 年)和武圣关羽(? －219年)的塑像。

A View of the Erlang God Temple It is the only temple in the whole area of the Eastern Qing Tombs. The Qing rulers ordered all temples be moved out when they decided to build tombs in the area. Because this temple had a small hill called "Monkey Hill" in front of it, it was left to appease the monkeys so that they would not make trouble for the dead. Worshipped in the temple today are the Erlang God, Lü Dong-bin, one of the Eight Immortals, and Guan Yu, an army general in ancient times.

二郎神像　二郎,中国神话传说中人物。一说他是战国时期(公元前 475－前 221 年)秦国蜀太守李冰的二儿子,帮助父亲治理岷江,修筑都江堰,因而被老百姓尊奉为神;一说是玉皇大帝的外甥杨戬,他有三只眼,手使三类两刃刀,活捉孙悟空。二郎庙中供奉的神像,就是杨戬,他威风凛凛,忠诚地为皇家看守着陵寝。

Statue of Erlang God　Erlang is a figure in a Chinese myth. Some people say he was the second son of Li Bing, governor of Sichuan during the Warring States Period (475-221 BC). He helped his father tame the Min River and build Dujiang Weir, and the local people took him as a god. Other people believe he was Yang Jian, nephew of the Jade Emperor, who had three eyes and caught the Monkey King. The Erlang worshipped in this temple is Yang Jiàn, who served as a guardian for the imperial tombs.

清东陵一瞥　清东陵共有单体建筑三百七十余座,五步一楼,十步一阁,依山隈,接云天,鸟鸣嘤嘤,流水潺潺,于幽静典雅之中,寓雄奇壮观之势。

A Bird's-Eye View of the Eastern Qing Tombs　All together there are more than 370 individual buildings in 14 independent cemetery compounds in the Eastern Qing Tombs. With birds singing and rivers running gurgling by, the place is extremely beautiful.

清 东 陵
THE EASTERN QING TOMBS

水口子

大坝

后龙台

乾宝山

瑞

CHANGRUI

万年沟

孝陵
Xiaoling Tomb

孝陵神道碑亭
Stele Pavilion

定东陵(慈安、慈禧)
Dingdong
(Ci'an, Cixi)
Tombs

裕妃园寝
Yufei Tomb

定妃园寝
Dingfei Tomb

裕陵
Yuling Tomb

定陵
Dingling Tomb

中国国际
China Intern

裕陵神道碑亭
Stele Pavilion

定陵神道碑亭
Stele Pavilion

清东陵文物保管所
Administrative Office

外宾接待站 Zun
Foreign Guest
Reception Centre

定陵牌楼门
Archway

停车场
Parking Lot

裕陵
Arch

定陵石像生
Stone Statues

旅游饭店
Taurist Rastaurant

五孔神道桥

五孔神道桥

裕陵
Arch

老新立

定大村

裕大村

裕陵
圣德神功碑亭
Stele Pavilion

河北村

谢家营

山东

西

南场

河南村

大

滦河

北京
Beijing

河

北

河

大

天津
Tianjin

清东陵
The Eastern Qing Tombs

漳沱

运

石家庄
Shijiazhuang

省

河

清东陵在河北省的位置
Map of Geographic Location of the
Eastern Qing Tombs in Hebei Province

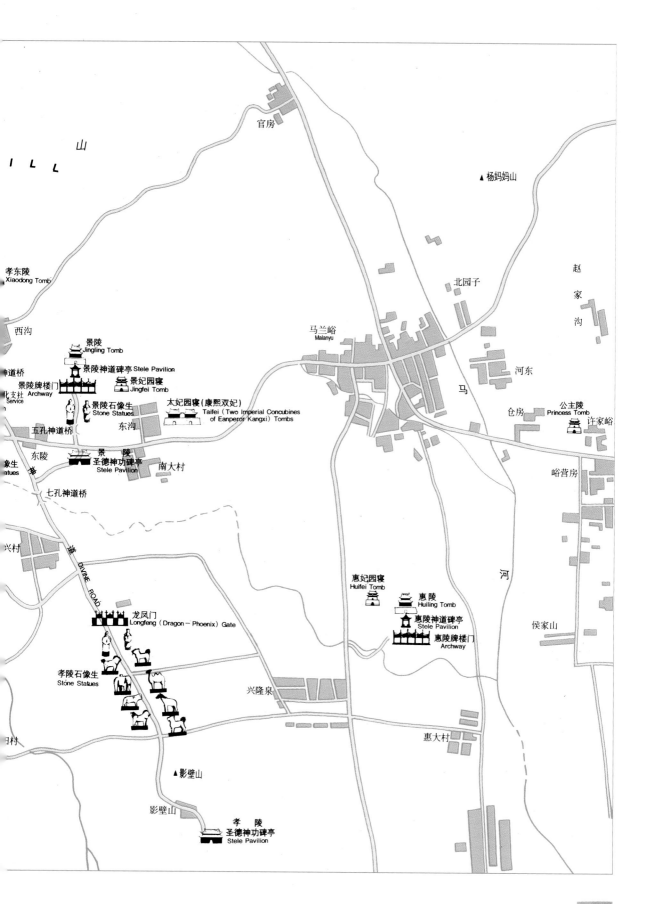

官房

山
LLL

▲杨妈妈山

赵
家
沟

孝东陵
Xiaodong Tomb

北园子

西沟

马兰峪
Malanyu

河东

马

神道桥

景陵
Jingling Tomb

景陵神道碑亭 Stele Pavilion

景陵牌楼门
Archway
化支社
Service

景妃园寝
Jingfei Tomb

公主陵
Princess Tomb

景陵石像生
Stone Statues

太妃园寝（康熙双妃）
Taifei (Two Imperial Concubines
of Eanperor Kangxi) Tombs

仓房

许家峪

五孔神道桥

东沟

象生
Statues

东陵

景   陵
圣德神功碑亭
Stele Pavilion

南大村

峪营房

七孔神道桥

惠妃园寝
Huifei Tomb

河

兴村

神
道
DIVINE ROAD

惠陵
Huiling Tomb

侯家山

龙凤门
Longfeng (Dragon - Phoenix) Gate

惠陵神道碑亭
Stele Pavilion

惠陵牌楼门
Archway

孝陵石像生
Stone Statues

兴隆泉

归村

惠大村

▲影壁山

影壁山

孝   陵
圣德神功碑亭
Stele Pavilion

各陵地宫内葬情况一览表

陵 名	所在地名	皇 帝	皇 后	皇 贵 妃
孝 陵		顺治皇帝	孝康章皇后佟佳氏 孝献皇后董鄂氏	
景 陵		康熙皇帝	孝诚仁皇后赫舍里氏 孝昭仁皇后钮祜禄氏 孝懿仁皇后佟佳氏 孝恭仁皇后乌雅氏	敬敏皇贵妃章佳氏
裕 陵	胜水峪	乾隆皇帝	孝贤纯皇后富察氏 孝仪纯皇后魏佳氏	慧贤皇贵妃高氏、哲悯皇贵妃富察氏、淑嘉皇贵妃金氏
定 陵	平安峪	咸丰皇帝	孝德显皇后萨克达氏	
惠 陵	双山峪	同治皇帝	孝哲毅皇后阿鲁特氏	
昭西陵			孝庄文皇后博尔济吉特氏	
孝东陵			孝惠章皇后博尔济吉特氏	
定东陵	普祥峪		孝贞显皇后钮祜禄氏	
定东陵	菩陀峪		孝钦显皇后叶赫那拉氏	

清 朝 皇 帝 世 系 表

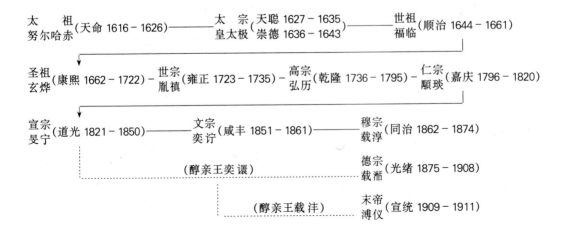

太　祖
努尔哈赤(天命 1616 - 1626)————太　宗(天聪 1627 - 1635
皇太极(崇德 1636 - 1643)————世祖
福临(顺治 1644 - 1661)

圣祖
玄烨(康熙 1662 - 1722)—世宗
胤禛(雍正 1723 - 1735)—高宗
弘历(乾隆 1736 - 1795)—仁宗
顒琰(嘉庆 1796 - 1820)

宣宗
旻宁(道光 1821 - 1850)————文宗
奕詝(咸丰 1851 - 1861)————穆宗
载淳(同治 1862 - 1874)

(醇亲王奕譞)　德宗
载湉(光绪 1875 - 1908)

(醇亲王载沣)　末帝
溥仪(宣统 1909 - 1911)

The Eastern Qing Tombs

Name of the Tomb	Emperor	Empress	Imperial Concubine
Xiaoling	Emperor Shun Zhi	Empresses Xiaokang Zhang and Xiaoxian	
Jingling	Emperor Kang Xi	Empresses Xiaocheng Ren, Xiaozhao Ren, Xiaoyi Ren and Xiaogong Ren	Imperial Concubine Jingmin
Yuling	Emperor Qian Long	Empresses Xiaoxian Chun and Xiaoyi Chun	Imperial Concubines Huixian, Zhemin and Shujia
Dingling	Emperor Xian Feng	Empress Xiaode Xian	
Huiling	Emperor Tong Zhi	Empress Xiaozhe Yi	
Western Zhaoling		Empress Xiaozhuang Wen	
Eastern Xiaoling		Empress Xiaohui Zhang	
Eastern Dingling		Empress Xiaozhen Xian	
Eastern Dingling		Empress Xiaoxin Xian	

Genealogical Table of the Qing Dynasty

Emperor Tai Zu (Nurhachi) (r. 1616 – 26) ———— Emperor Tai Zong (Huangtaiji) (r. 1627 – 43) ———— Emperor Shi Zu or Shun Zhi (Fu Lin) (r. 1644 – 61)

Emperor Sheng Zu or Kang Xi (Xuan Ye) (r. 1662 – 1722) — Emperor Shi Zong or Yong Zheng (Yin Zhen) (r. 1723 – 35) — Emperor Gao Zong or Qian Long (Hong Li) (r. 1736 – 95) — Emperor Ren Zong or Jia Qing (Yong Yan) (r. 1796 – 1820)

Emperor Xuan Zong or Dao Guang (Min Ning) (r. 1821 – 50) ———— Emperor Wen Zong or Xian Feng (Yi Ning) (r. 1851 – 61) ———— Emperor Mu Zong or Tong Zhi (Zai Chun) (r. 1862 – 74)

(Yi Xuan) .... Emperor De Zong or Guang Xu (Zai Tian) (r. 1875 – 1908)

(Zai Feng) .... Emperor Xuan Tong (Pu Yi) (r. 1909 – 11)

图书在版编目（CIP）数据

清东陵/李万贵，庞玉忠主编 . - 北京：中国世界语出版
社,1997.4
　ISBN 7－5052－0304－5

　I. 清… 　II.①李… 　②庞… 　III. 陵墓－中国－清代－画册
IV. K928.76－64

中国版本图书馆 CIP 数据核字（96）第 10400 号

《清东陵》编委会：

主　　编	李万贵　庞玉忠
副 主 编	李云森　李　生　尹庆林
	刘会奇　晏子友　徐广源
文字撰写	晏子友
责任编辑	施永南　望天星
摄　　影	望天星　罗文发　董宗贵
	徐广源　熊井牧勇(日)
	王金辉　王春树　董大明
装帧设计	望天星
封面题字	安　斌

清东陵

*

中国世界语出版社出版

北京 1201 厂印刷

中国国际图书贸易总公司(国际书店)发行

（中国北京车公庄西路 35 号）

北京邮政信箱第 399 号　邮政编码 100044

1997 年(16 开)第一版第一次印刷

ISBN 7－5052－0304－5/K·57(外)

05500

85－CE－380P

Editing Committee of *The Eastern Qing Tombs*
Editors-in-chief: Li Wangui and Pang Yuzhong
Deputy editors-in-chief: Li Yunsen, Li Sheng, Yin Qinglin,
    Liu Huiqi, Yan Ziyou and Xu Guangyuan
Text by: Yan Ziyou
Editors: Shi Yongnan and Wang Tianxing
Photos: Wang Tianxing, Luo Wenfa, Dong Zonggui,
    Xu Guangyuan, Kumai Bokuyu, Wang Jinhui,
    Wang Chunshu and Dong Daming
Design: Wang Tianxing